# *Gallery*

*for Pamela Sztybel*

I slid past a pencil drawing of a young girl,
a white marble statue of a warrior,
and a vase that no one had dropped
in over five thousand years of human history.

Then I stopped at an oil painting
in a frame flecked with gold,
which I gazed at for such a long time
that the painting began to look back at me,

which was especially odd because this
was not a portrait but a landscape,
and what was looking back at me was a pale field,
a stand of trees, and a blue and light orange sky.

The longer we looked at one another
the more it seemed like one of those staring contests
you can never win, the kind you might
get into with a dog with bangs over its eyes.

But then the painting blinked,
or at least a tiny cow I had not noticed
changed her expression, and that was enough
to return me to the world beyond the painting

which now was textured like a fabric,
finely threaded and grained with color,
as if a brush had been lifted by a hand
and pressed, again and again, against its surface.

Billy Collins

Published in the United States of America in 2008 by
Spanierman Gallery, LLC, 45 East 58th Street, New York, NY 10022.



ISBN 0-945936-89-3

Design: Light Blue Studio
Photography: Roz Akin
Color separations: Center Page
Lithography: Meridian Printing

# *Pamela Sztybel*

## RECENT LANDSCAPES

September 4–October 4, 2008

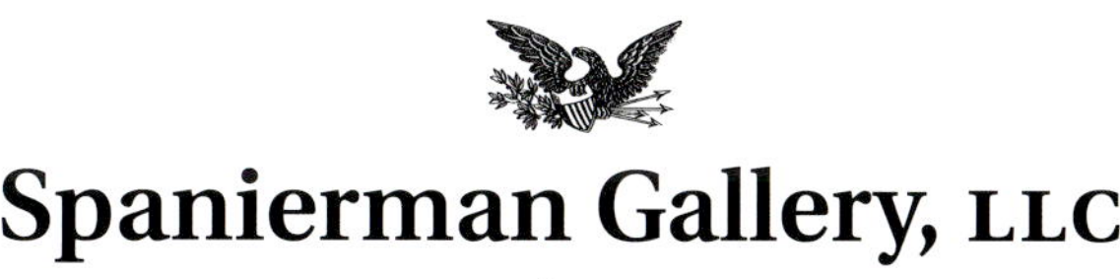

**Spanierman Gallery, LLC**
www.spanierman.com

45 East 58th Street New York, NY 10022 Tel (212) 832-0208 christineberry@spanierman.com
Gallery hours: Monday through Saturday 9:30 to 5:30

Although certainly unintentional, Pamela Sztybel's last name seems eerily convergent with her art. It is difficult if not impossible to pronounce all of its letters together, yet they form a melodious sound when spoken. Her paintings have a similar quality of elusive mystery, in which we often cannot differentiate their parts. They form harmonious totalities of experience, unified more by light and shadow than by the arrangement of distinct motifs. Produced through the filter of memory, Sztybel's works depict sites whose details are forgotten, so that only shape and tone remain. At the same time, they are meta-images that consider why we are drawn to looking at nature, what we seek in it and derive from it.

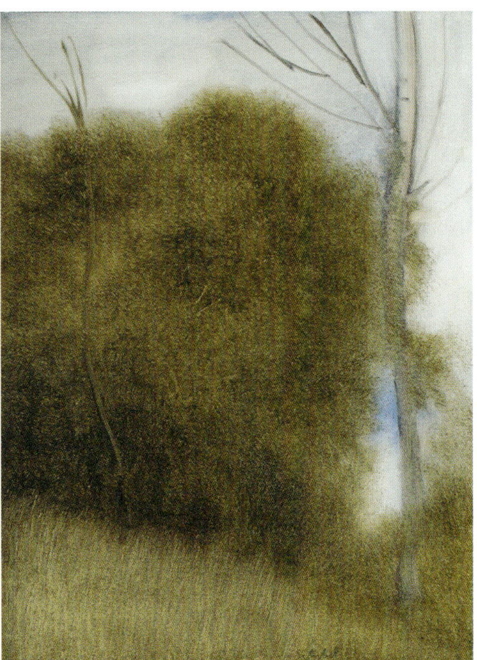

Fig. 1.
*After Seeing a Salt Print by Corot*, 2008
oil on paper mounted on board, 17 × 12¾ inches

With their blurred edges and serene luminescence, they ponder the cross-cultural notion that nature can be reviving and calming. They ask whether the answer is simply that natural places enable us to escape from civilization and its stresses or, more profoundly, as suggested by Simon Schama, to express the "craving to find in nature a consolation for our mortality," which Schama suggests may be the reason "why groves of trees, with the annual promise of spring awakening, are thought to be a fitting décor for our earthly remains."[1] In *Landscape and Memory*, a consideration of how the veins of myth and memory lie beneath our "conventional sight level," Schama observes: "So the mystery behind this commonplace turns out to be eloquent on the deepest relationships between natural form and human design."[2] Sztybel's paintings probe the yearning that is one of the most powerful and universal: our desire for a connection with nature.

Tellingly Sztybel has titled one of her works, *After Seeing a Salt Print by Corot* (Fig. 1). Her reference is to the clichés-verre (or "hand-drawn negatives") by Camille Corot, created by scratching soot-covered glass plates and placing them face down on light-sensitive paper. Part print, part photograph, such images resulted in the softening of forms without the loss of their essential compositions. When printed, these images were often inverted, producing depictions that parry tenuously between a mirroring of the visible world and an emanation of the artist's shaping perception. Sztybel's title reveals her interest in exploring the many ways in which what we see outside ourselves reflects our inner experience and how we discern and bring to it its form, beauty, and capacity to provide what we need. By alluding to Corot, she also denotes the way that the art of the past affects our vision, whether consciously or not, evoking structures and associations linked with myths and ideas that have evolved over time, their sources often forgotten.

The spirit of George Inness presides in Sztybel's *Golden* (Cat. 6). Inness's association of the misty, dimming light of dusk with a spiritual presence beyond the visible world is similarly made by Szytbel yet without a religious implication. Here the heaviness of the atmosphere seems to weigh down the foliage, yet the artist provides a force of relief and rejuvenation in the golden light of the sunset that radiates from the v-shaped opening between trees and draws our gaze upward.

In *Low Moon* (Cat. 16) Szytbel's subject is the shimmer of moonlight. Employing a sfumato approach that harks back to Leonardo da Vinci, she blends her tones so softly that transitions are imperceptible, creating a sense of depth and volume within the picture plane along with a feeling of mystery and anticipation. In the transformative glow of the light, we can imagine the stirring of a night of magical revelry.

There are associations with Andrew Wyeth in *Side with No Windows* (Cat. 12). The large gabled form centrally located in the painting is synonymous with domestic life. However, the view of a side wall devoid of windows, with an indistinct opening at its base, seems thwarting, mute, and incomplete. It evokes less the reality of a home than of the sense of a desire to see and bring one into focus, so as to accept its offering of shelter and comfort. The house is only distinguished from the sky by its clear outline, making it seem drawn into a landscape rather than actually existing within it. A blue dot of paint at its left edge further signifies the role of the artist's hand in the creating of the image, yet the hazy trees and grass nestle around the structure and ask us to accept its reality in the landscape.

In *Someone's Barn* (Cat. 10) our gaze is far across a meadow where a building is vaguely discernible amid similarly toned trees. Here, the feeling is of a locale whose identity for us is shaped by our remote experience of it. We recognize it as "something off in the distance beyond the open fields" rather than as somewhere with which we are familiar from having seen it close up. Its presence is a reminder of the way that few places in nature, for better or worse, are untouched by human modification.

*Towpath* (Cat. 13) expresses a similar but more poignant perspective. Here the cleared, sunlit path draws our eye quickly through the green landscape. It is only on noting the title of the work that we become aware of the waterway at the left, now thin due to overgrowth and too shallow for the towing of boats—the reason the path was created and once had a purpose. That the path remains well-tended, even while it no longer serves its original function, reflects the way that the past leaves its presence behind, affecting our experience of a place, whether we are aware of the imprint of history on it or not. At the same time, perhaps the feeling of pleasure in traveling along such routes is sparked by a vague desire to connect with a time gone by, even if evidence of that earlier era has vanished. The painting is also a reminder of how nostalgia itself can create its own new mapping.

In both *Through an Opening* (Cat. 3) and *Going By* (Cat. 15) Sztybel uses the structure of the "cathedral grove," recalling images by Hudson River School artists such as Asher B. Durand and Worthington Whittredge. The aperture in the trees has associations with the pagan primitive grove and from it the creation of the Gothic arch through which divine light flowed. Such a history explains why we are drawn to look through these portholes and why the tiny white sail of a boat holds our interest and perhaps our veneration.

In several striking monochromatic paintings in the exhibition, Sztybel explores subtle gradations of light and shadow. In the spreading darkness in *Willow I* (Cat. 5) the faint remaining light illuminates the contours and textures of forms. In *Light Trunk* (Cat. 17) we are situated under a large dark tree that fills the composition. Through the dense leaves, the persistence of the daylight gives spectral life to the trunk before us, evoking a sense of enchantment. In *On a Slope* (Cat. 2) the day is ending, while a white farmhouse on the hillside brings the richness of the grays and blacks in the landscape into relief. The neutral palette of these paintings adds to the quiet, soothing feeling they elicit, while their appeal is probably due to how they conjure the sensuous qualities of landscape photography before the invention of color processing.

Sztybel often focuses a work on a detail or unexpected quality in a landscape, the patch of sky in *Blue Corner* (Cat. 8), the white flowers in *A Few Blossoms on a Dull Day* (Cat. 1), the presence of fall foliage in a single tree in *Early Red* (Cat. 4), and the subtle intensification of light signaling an approaching storm in *In Front* (Cat. 18). These works reveal Sztybel's awareness of how feeling and cognition affect the way we see and bring to a landscape as much meaning and beauty as may exist innately within it. *Where We Went Walking* (Cat. 11) exemplifies her vision. While the path leads into the countryside, it is clear from the title and the perspective in the work that Sztybel's viewpoint is looking backward along the route she and a companion have already traveled. The uptilted perspective urges a turning forward away from the landscape, which will soon be behind the artist, leaving us with the memory of her passage.

Lisa N. Peters

1. Simon Schama, *Landscape and Memory* (New York: Alfred A. Knopf, 1995), 14.
2. Schama, *Landscape and Memory*, 14.

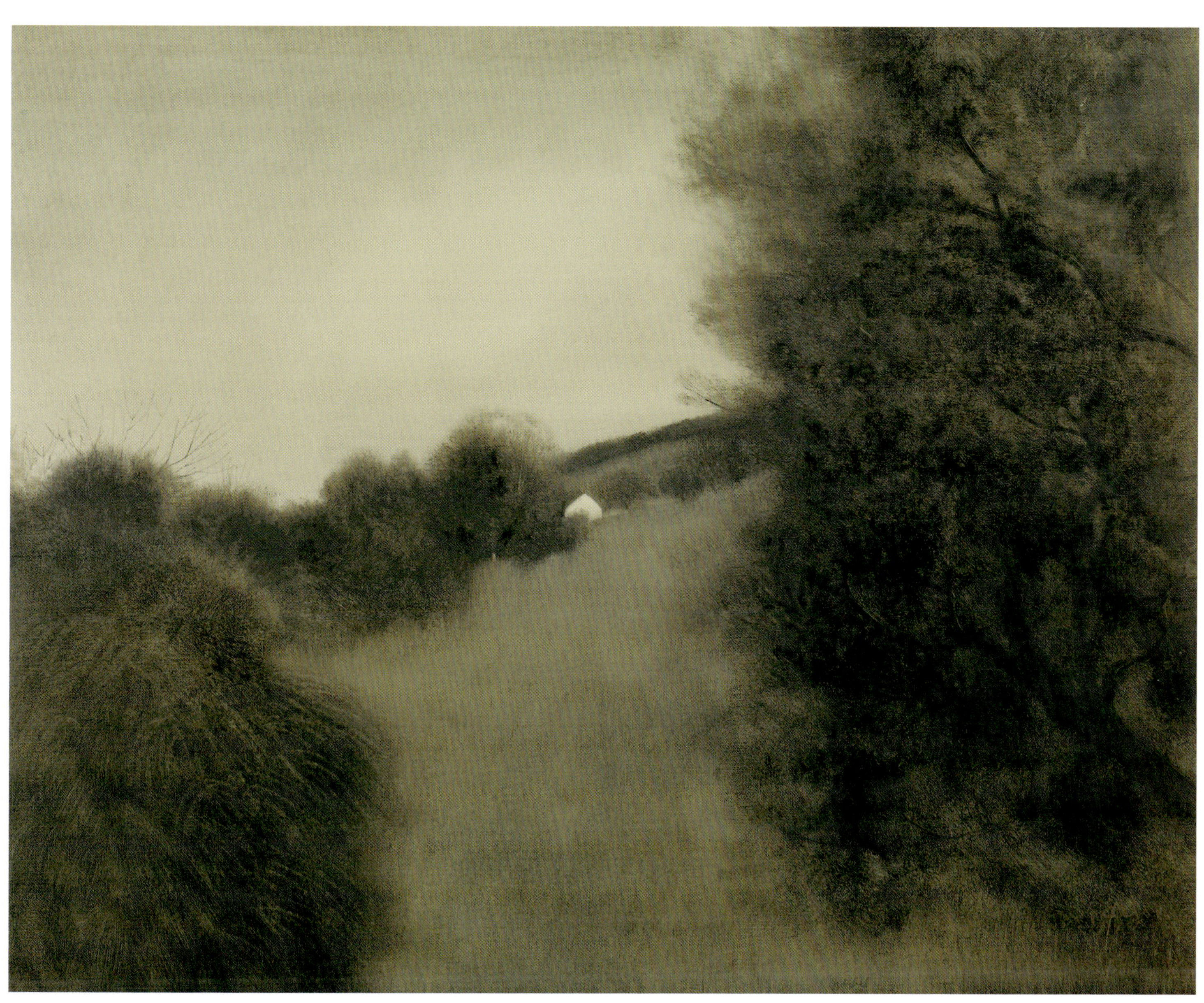

2. *On a Slope*, 2008, oil on textured paper mounted on board, 30½ × 37 inches

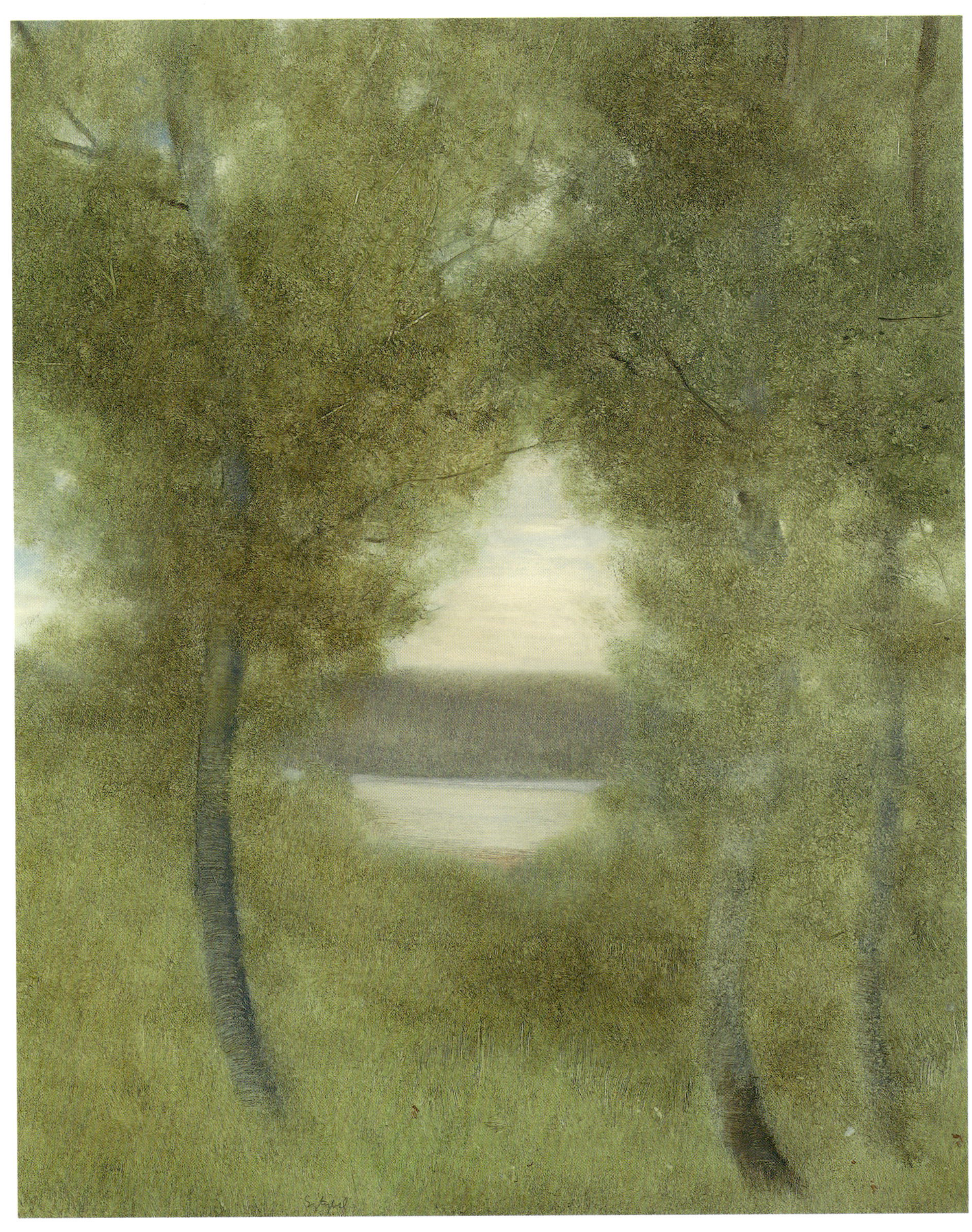

3. *Through an Opening*, 2008, oil on paper mounted on board, 29¾ × 24 inches

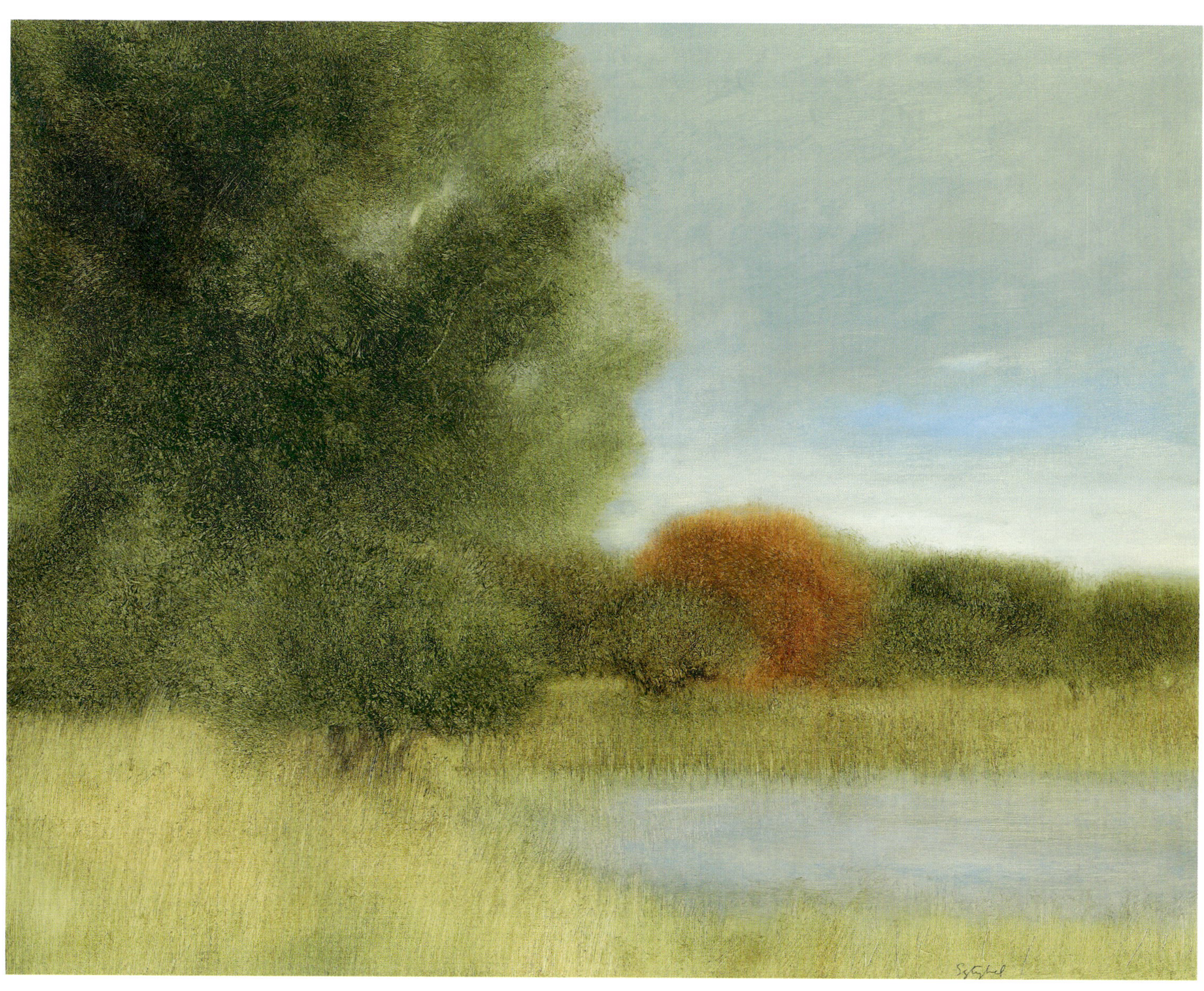

4. *Early Red*, 2008, oil on paper mounted on board, 18¾ × 23¼ inches

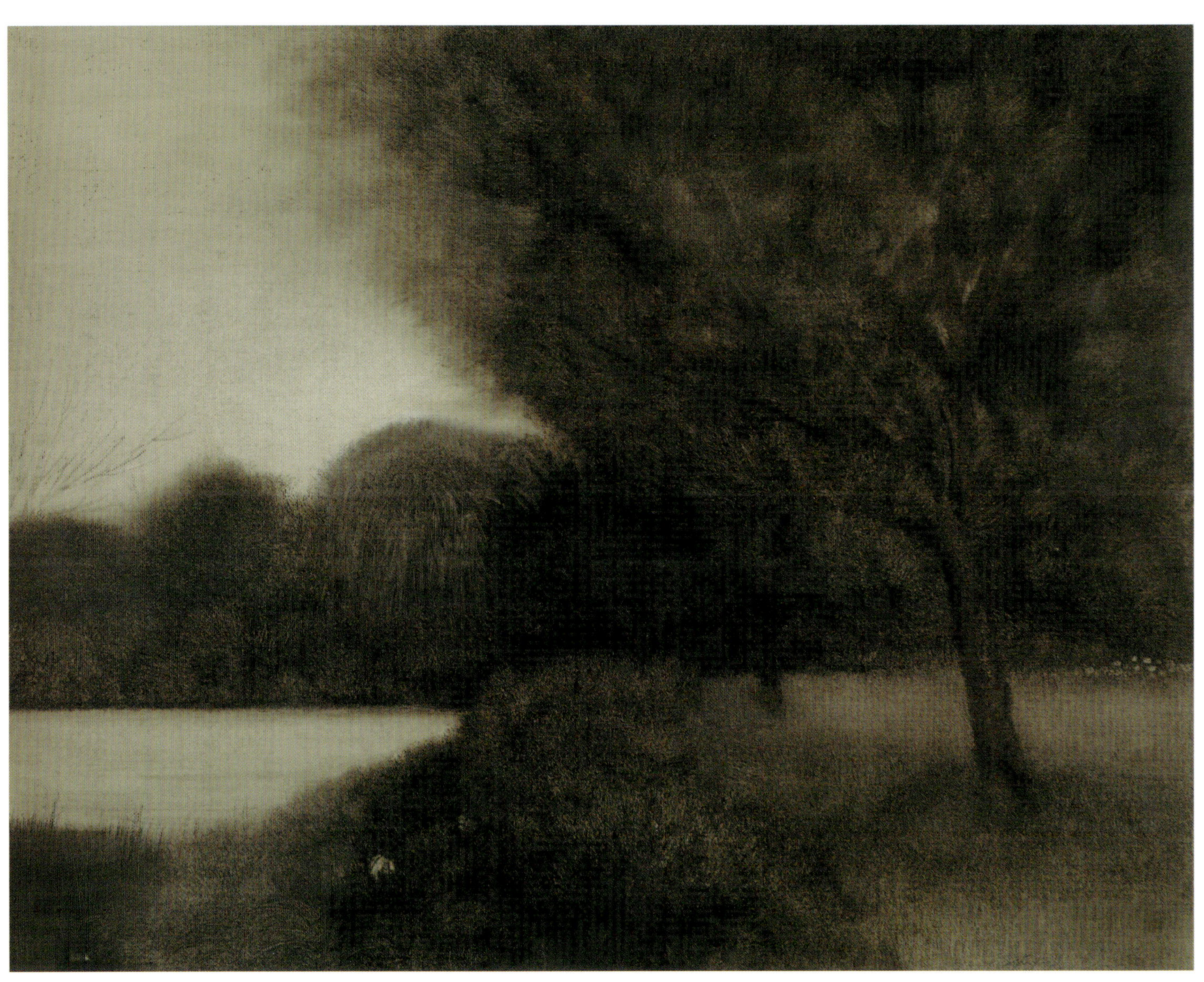

5. *Willow I*, 2008, oil on textured paper mounted on board, 20 × 24½ inches

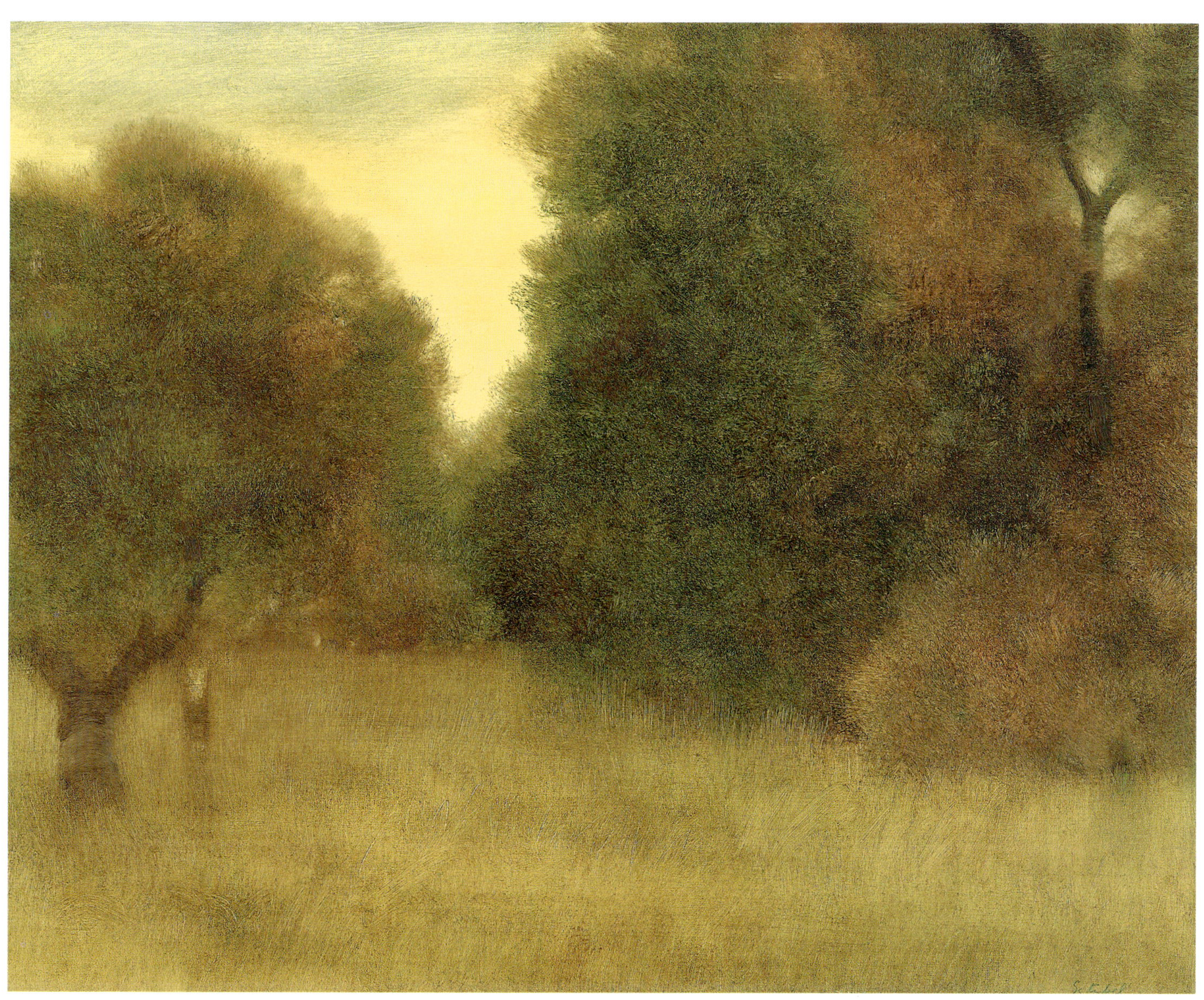

6. *Golden*, 2008, oil on paper mounted on board, 16¼ × 20 inches

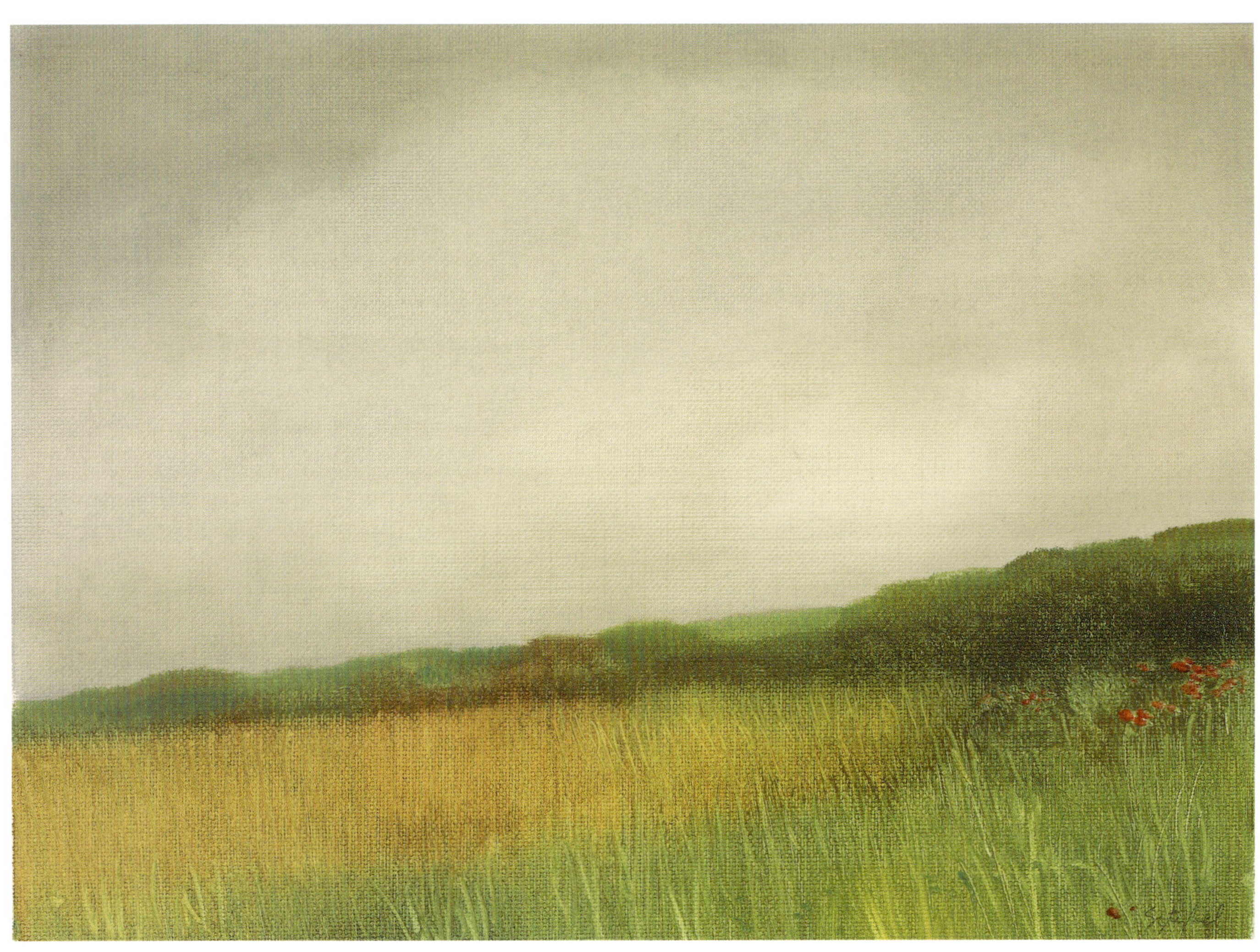

7. *Dry Field*, 2008, oil on textured paper mounted on board, 9¾ × 13 inches

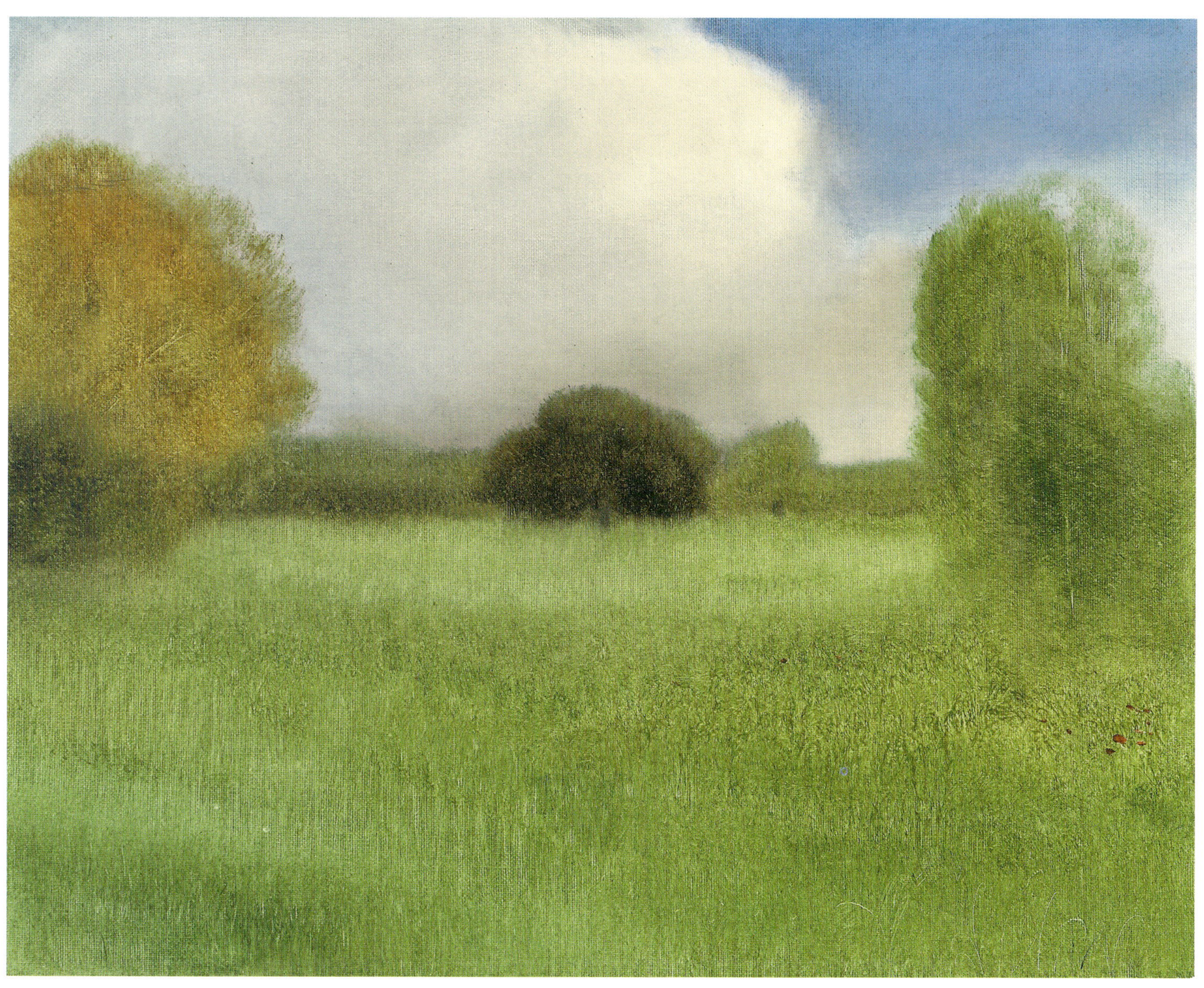

8. *Blue Corner*, 2008, oil on textured paper mounted on board, 16½ × 20½ inches

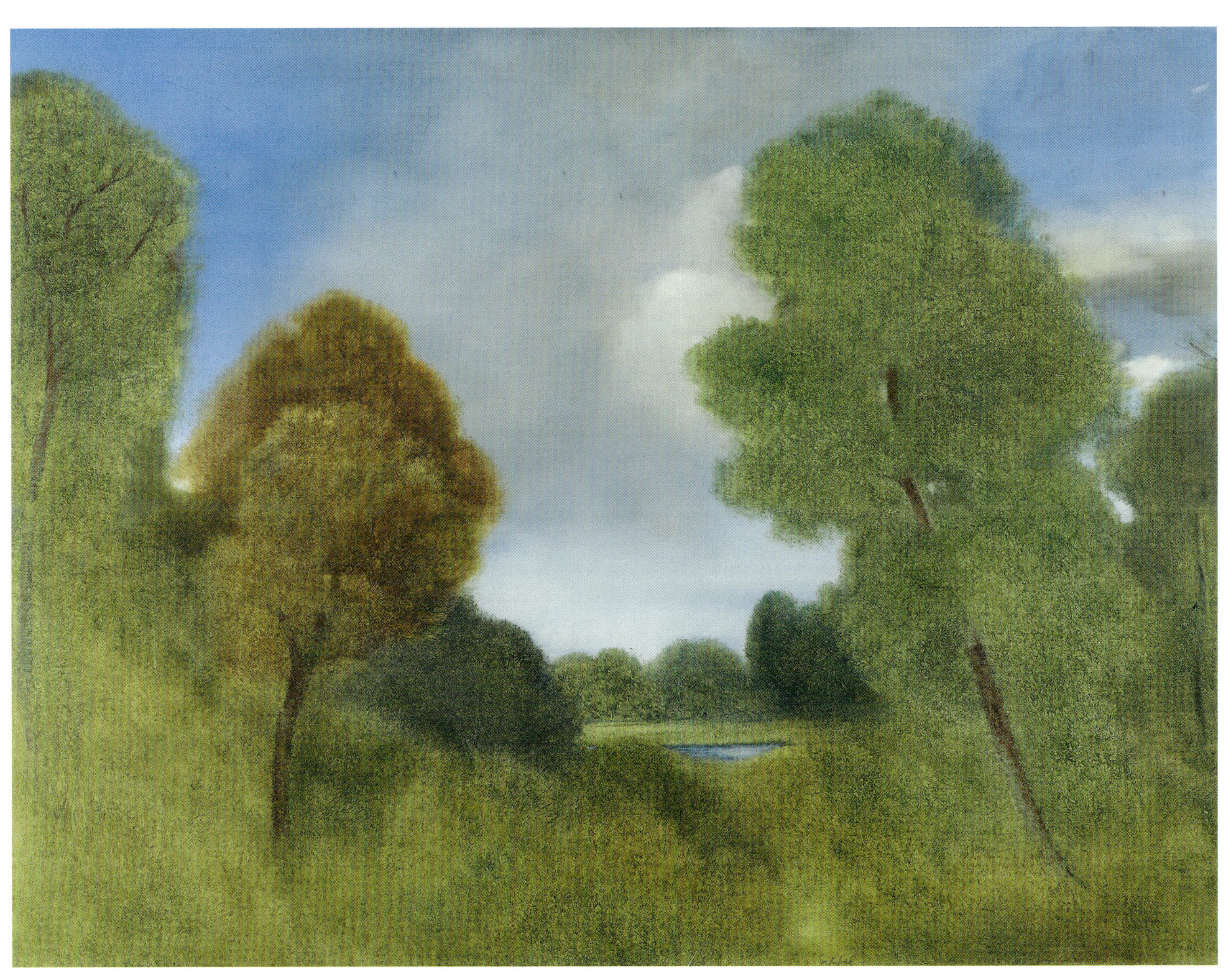

9. *Moving Through*, 2008, oil on textured paper mounted on board, 33½ × 43 inches

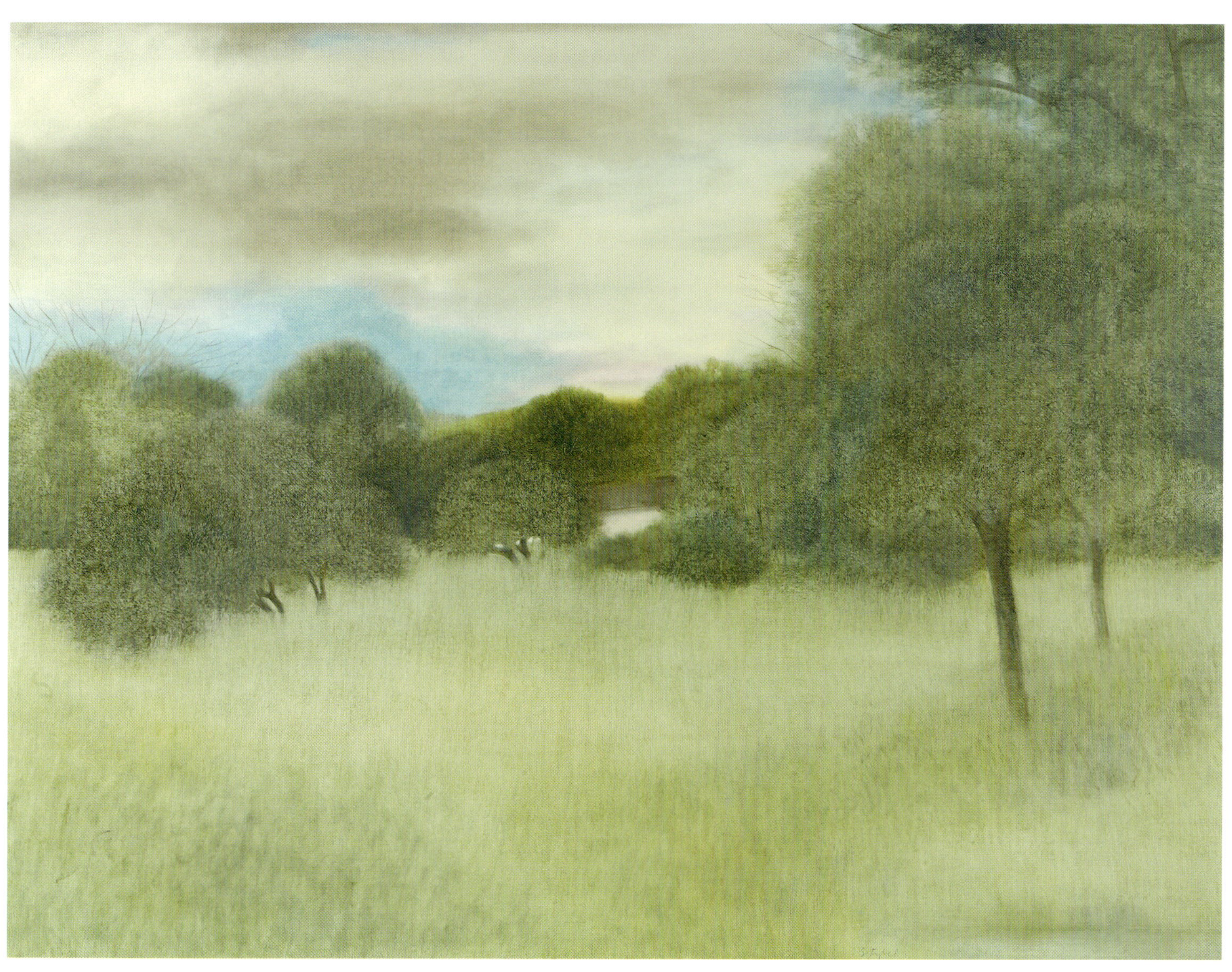

10. *Someone's Barn*, 2008, oil on textured paper mounted on board, 33¼ × 43 inches

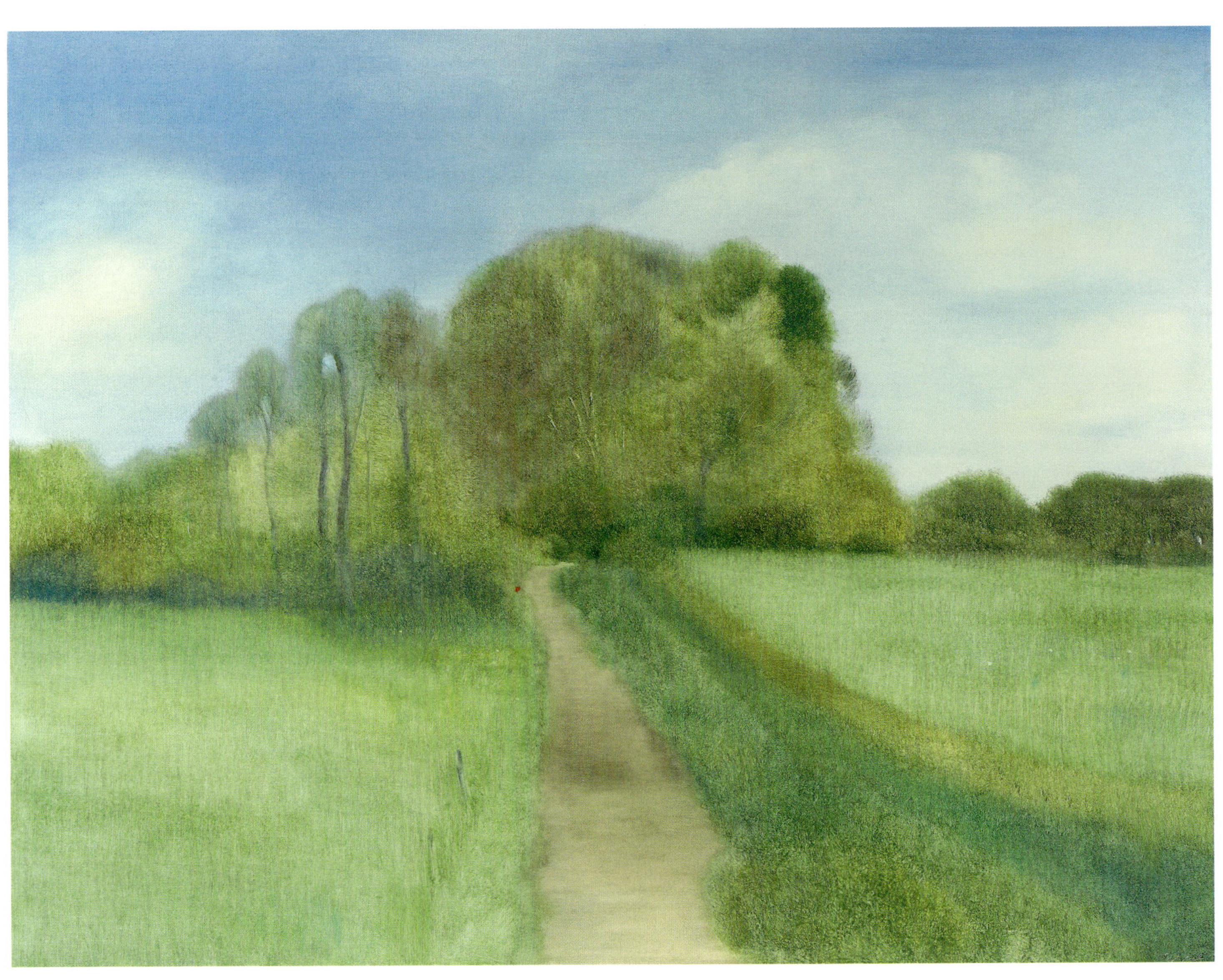

11. *Where We Went Walking*, 2008, oil on textured paper mounted on board, 33 × 42 inches

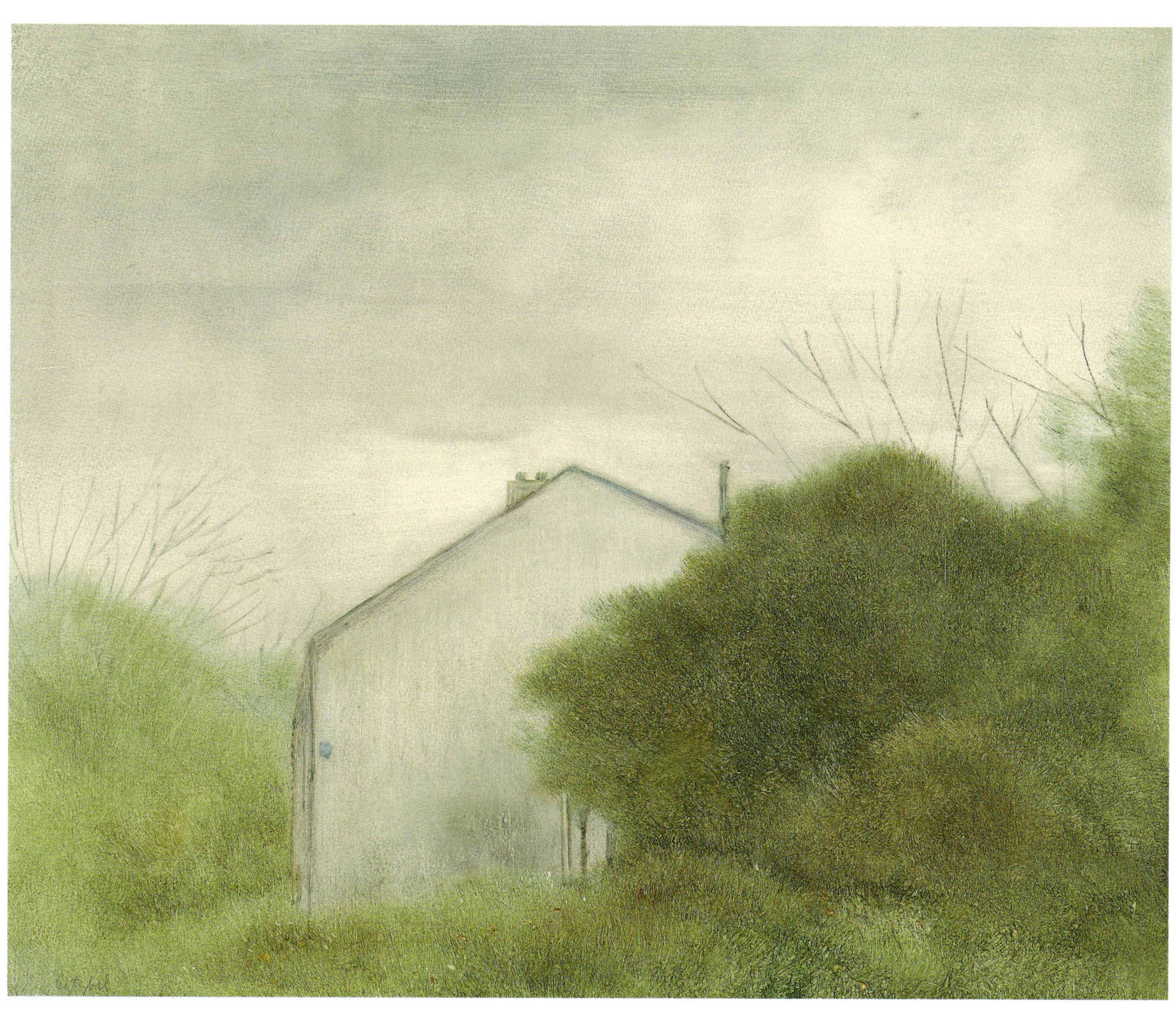

12. *Side with No Windows*, 2008, oil on paper mounted on board, 17 × 20 inches

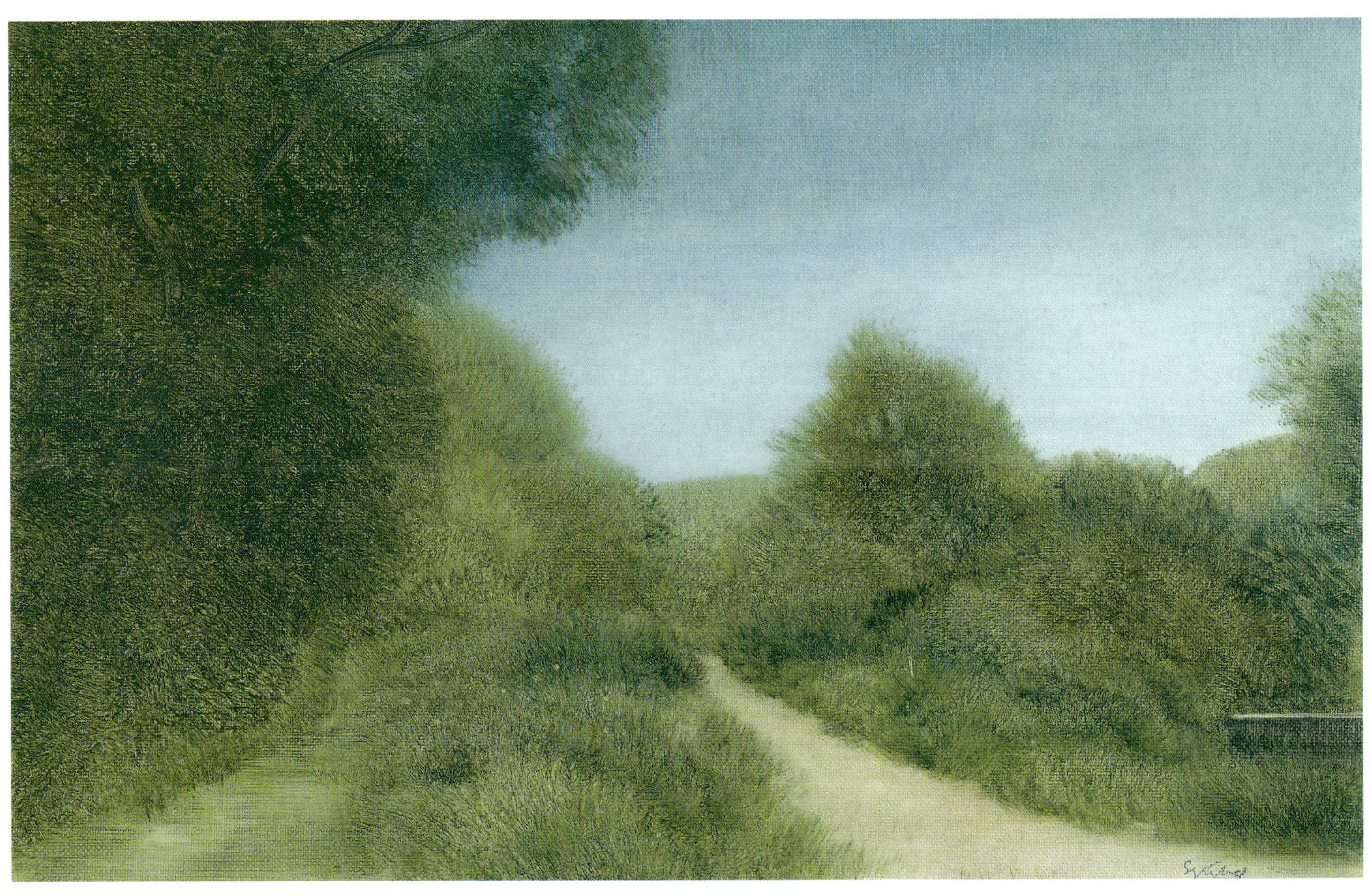

13. *Towpath*, 2008, oil on textured paper mounted on board, 11¼ × 17½ inches

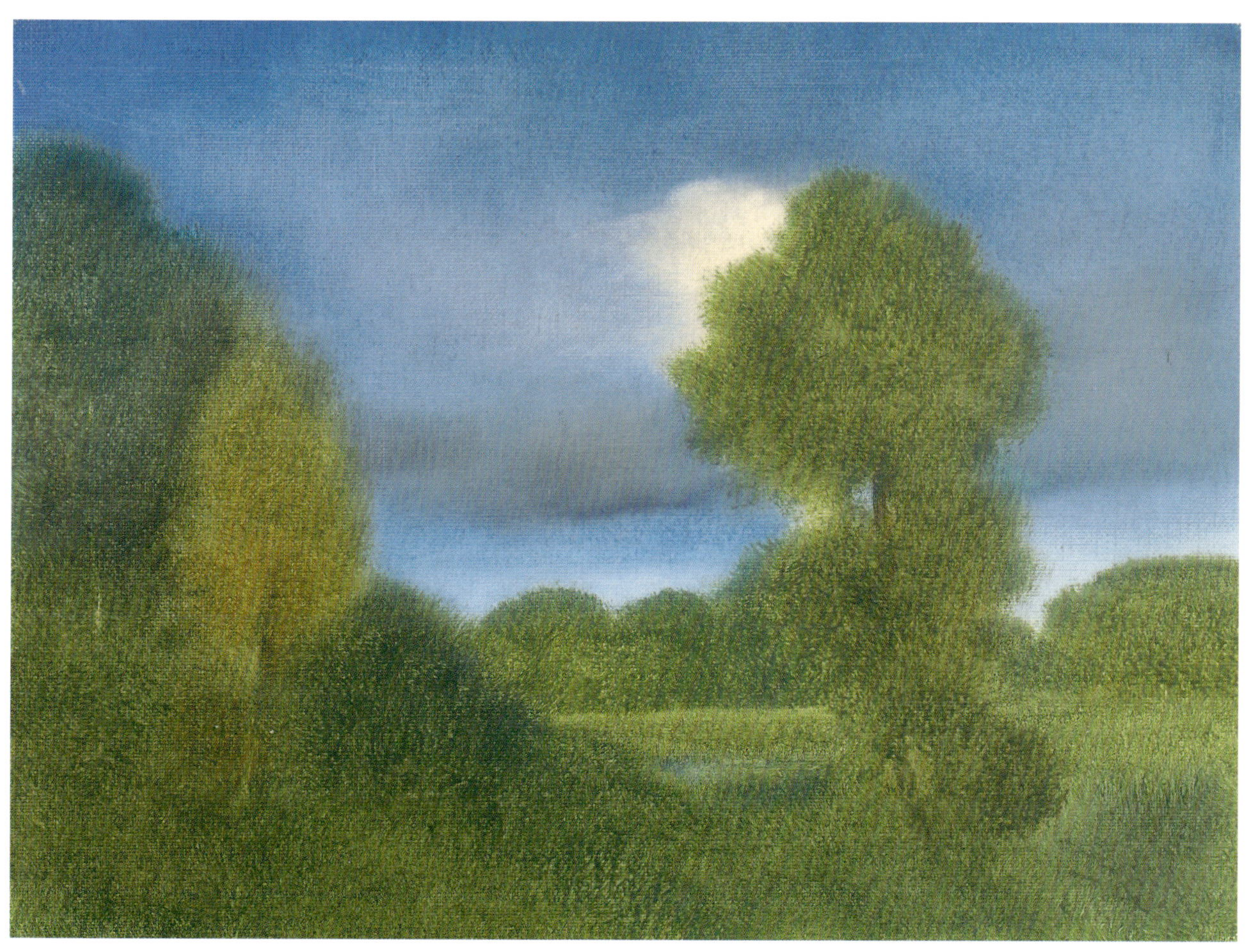

14. *Study for* Moving Through, 2008, oil on textured paper mounted on board, 11¾ × 15¾ inches

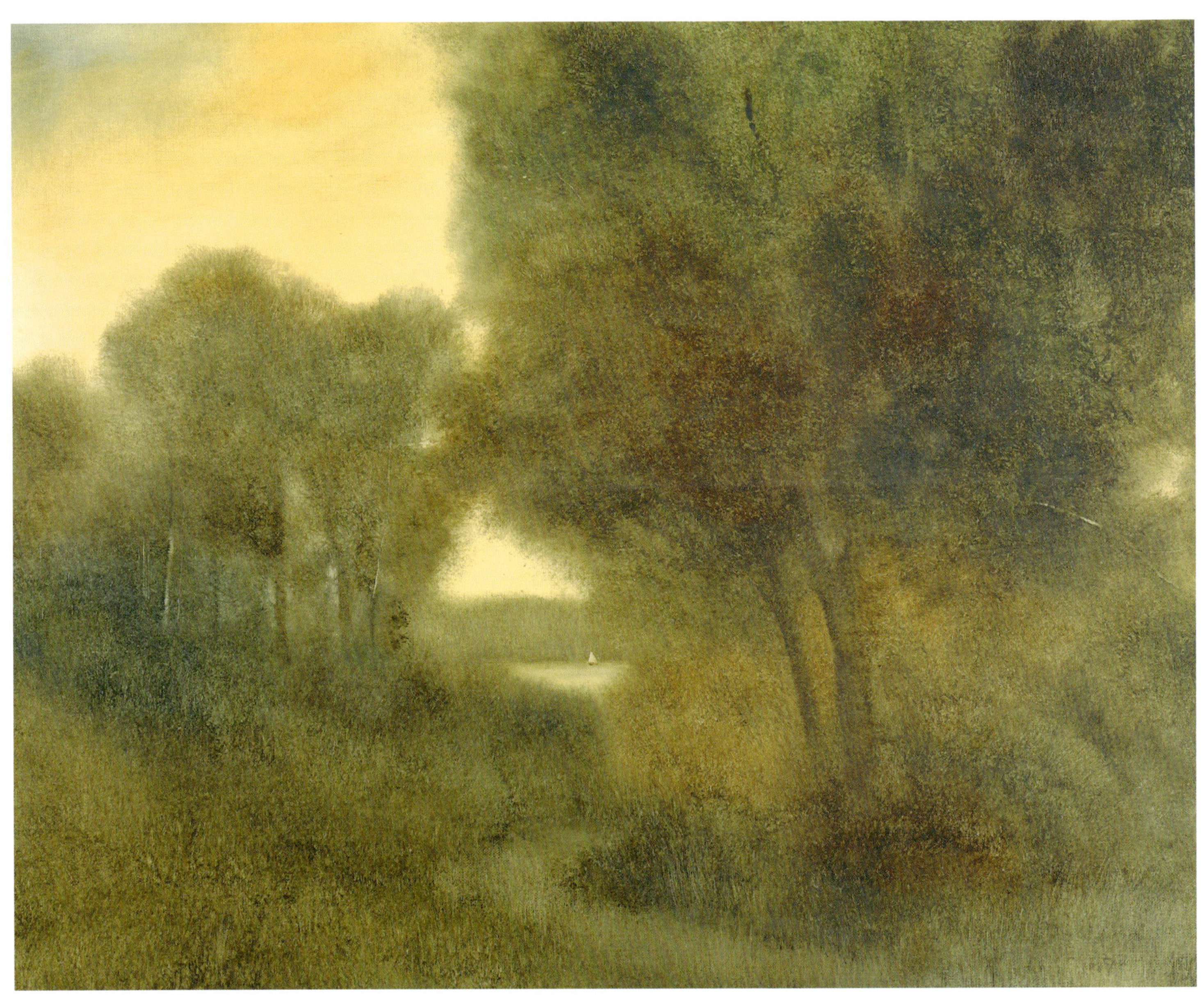

15. *Going By*, 2008, oil on textured paper mounted on board, 24¾ × 30½ inches

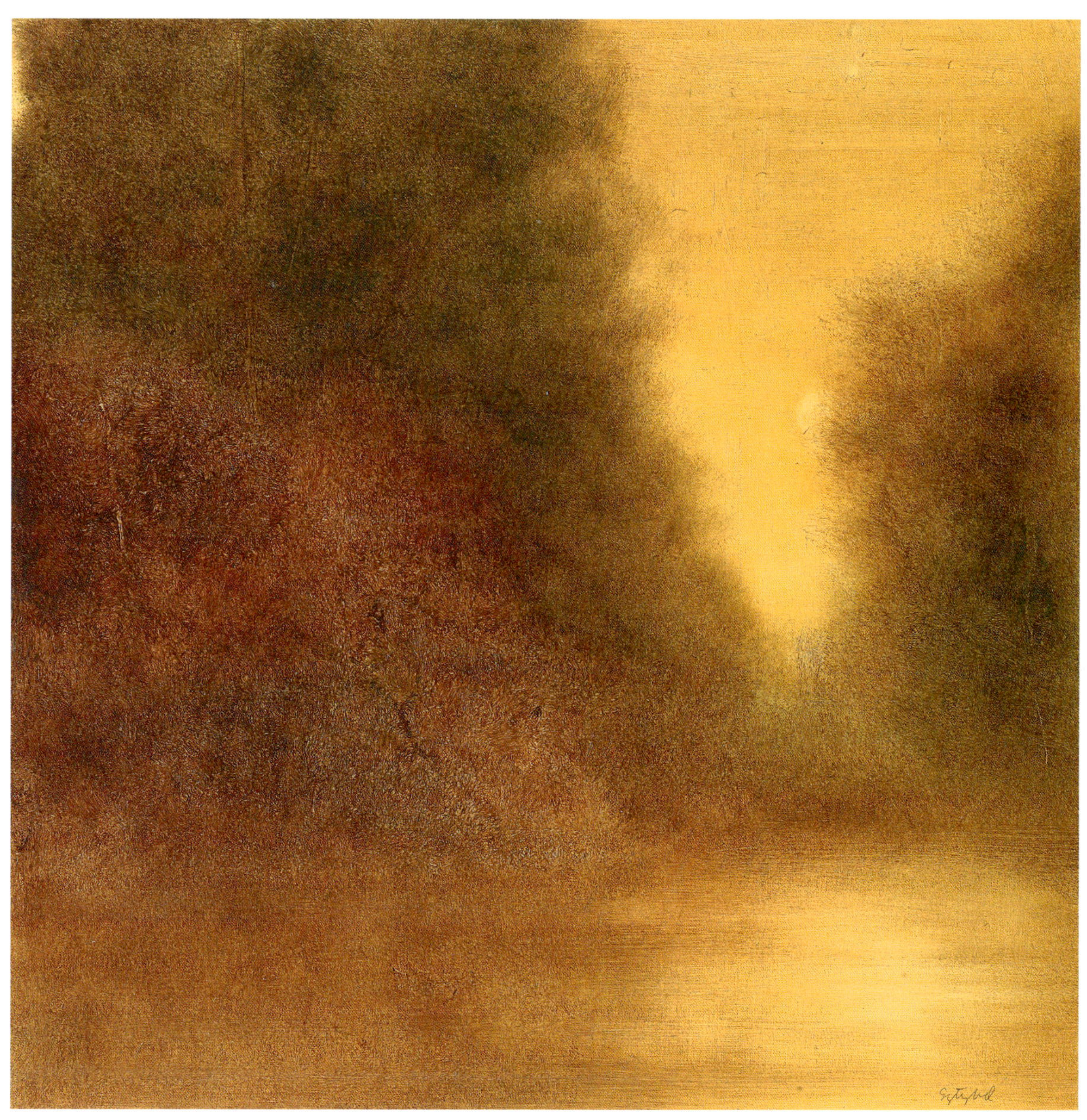

16. *Low Moon,* 2008, oil on paper mounted on board, 21¼ × 21 inches

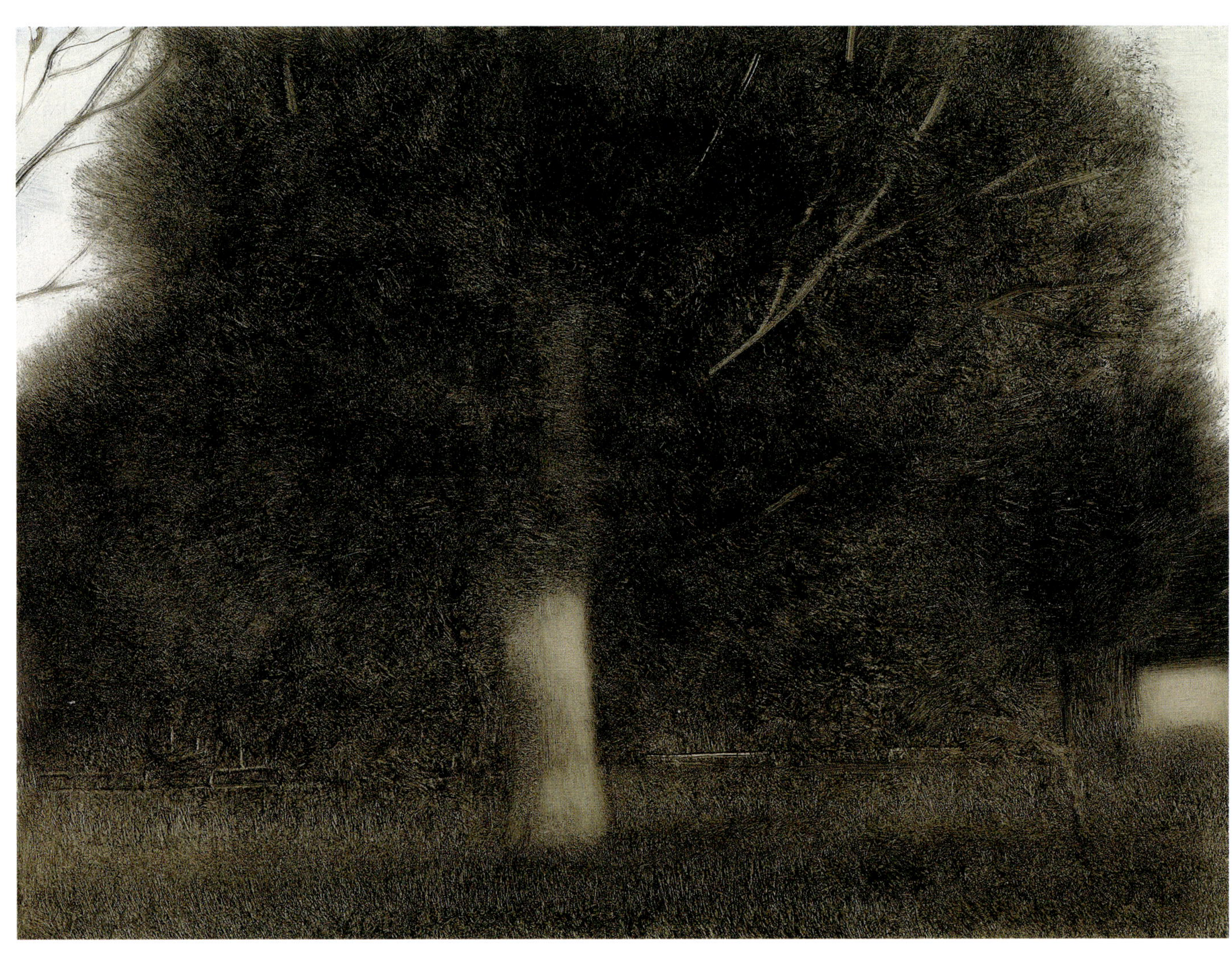

17. *Light Trunk*, 2008, oil on paper mounted on board, 9¾ × 13 inches

# *Checklist of Works in the Exhibition*

*After Seeing a Salt Print by Corot,* 2008 (Fig. 1)
Oil on paper mounted on board
17 × 12¾ inches

*Another Summer,* 2008
Oil on paper mounted on board
22¾ × 21¼ inches

*Beginning of Change,* 2008
Oil on paper mounted on board
18 × 23¼ inches

*Beyond the Mountain Place,* 2008
Oil on paper mounted on board
40 × 60 inches

*Blue Corner,* 2008 (Cat. 8)
Oil on textured paper mounted on board
16½ × 20½ inches

*Blue Sky, Bowed Hill,* 2008
Oil on textured paper mounted on board
22¾ × 27¼ inches

*Cooler Air Coming In,* 2006
Oil on linen
31¼ × 45¾ inches

*Distant Hill,* 2008
Oil on paper mounted on board
18¾ × 22 inches

*Dry Field,* 2008 (Cat. 7)
Oil on textured paper mounted on board
9¾ × 13 inches

*Early Red,* 2008 (Cat. 4)
Oil on paper mounted on board
18¾ × 23¼ inches

*Edge of the Field,* 2008
Oil on paper mounted on board
16 × 20 inches

*Fence,* 2008
Oil on textured paper mounted on board
8½ × 10 inches

*A Few Blossoms on a Dull Day,* 2008 (Cat. 1)
Oil on textured paper mounted on board
23¾ × 30½ inches

*Filled Space,* 2008
Oil on paper mounted on board
9 × 12 inches

*Full,* 2008
Oil on textured paper mounted on board
12 × 14½ inches

*Going By,* 2008 (Cat. 15)
Oil on textured paper mounted on board
24¾ × 30½ inches

*Golden,* 2008 (Cat. 6)
Oil on paper mounted on board
16¼ × 20 inches

*Grazing Place,* 2008
Oil on textured paper mounted on board
34 × 45½ inches

*Half Pond,* 2008
Oil on textured paper mounted on board
15½ × 18½ inches

*Hedge,* 2008
Oil on textured paper mounted on board
26 × 31 inches

*Hillside,* 2008
Oil on textured paper mounted on board
16¼ × 18¼ inches

*Housatonic,* 2008
Oil on paper mounted on board
12¾ × 17 inches

*Housatonic II,* 2008
Oil on paper mounted on board
19½ × 25¾ inches

*In Close,* 2008
Oil on linen mounted on board
12 × 14½ inches

*In Close and Overgrown*, 2008
Oil on textured paper mounted on board
23¼ × 33½ inches

*In Front*, 2008 (Cat. 18)
Oil on paper mounted on board
35¼ × 45¼ inches

*Leafed Out*, 2008
Oil on textured paper mounted on board
11 × 16½ inches

*Light Trunk*, 2008 (Cat. 17)
Oil on paper mounted on board
9¾ × 13 inches

*Low Moon*, 2008 (Cat. 16)
Oil on paper mounted on board
21¼ × 21 inches

*Low Moon II*, 2008
Oil on paper mounted on board
9⅞ × 9¼ inches

*Moving Through*, 2008 (Cat. 9)
Oil on textured paper mounted on board
33½ × 43 inches

*Night Field*, 2008
Oil on paper mounted on board
10½ × 12½ inches

*Not Yet Mowed*, 2008
Oil on paper mounted on board
16 × 21¾ inches

*On a Slope*, 2008 (Cat. 2)
Oil on textured paper mounted on board
30½ × 37 inches

*Pool*, 2008
Oil on paper mounted on board
15¾ × 20 inches

*Possibility of Rain*, 2008
Oil on textured paper mounted on board
9¾ × 11¼ inches

*Shed*, 2008
Oil on textured paper mounted on board
14 × 16¼ inches

*Side with No Windows*, 2008 (Cat. 12)
Oil on paper mounted on board
17 × 20 inches

*Someone's Barn*, 2008 (Cat. 10)
Oil on textured paper mounted on board
33¼ × 43 inches

*Study for* Going By, 2008
Oil on textured paper mounted on board
10 × 12¼ inches

*Study for* In Close, 2008
Oil on paper mounted on board
9½ × 10¾ inches

*Study for* Moving Through, 2008 (Cat. 14)
Oil on textured paper mounted on board
11¾ × 15¾ inches

*Tall and Thin*, 2008
Oil on paper mounted on board
18½ × 20¼ inches

*Through an Opening*, 2008 (Cat. 3)
Oil on paper mounted on board
29¾ × 24 inches

*Towpath*, 2008 (Cat. 13)
Oil on textured paper mounted on board
11¼ × 17½ inches

*Turquoise Outbuilding*, 2008
Oil on textured paper mounted on board
19¾ × 23 inches

*Violet Ribbon*, 2008
Oil on paper mounted on board
16¼ × 19½ inches

*The Way Out*, 2008
Oil on textured paper mounted on board
18¾ × 14¼ inches

*Where We Went Walking*, 2008 (Cat. 11)
Oil on textured paper mounted on board
33 × 42 inches

*Willow I*, 2008 (Cat. 5)
Oil on textured paper mounted on board
20 × 24½ inches

*Willow II*, 2008
Oil on textured paper mounted on board
32¼ × 40¼ inches

**A price list is available upon request.**